RIVER FOREST PUBLIC LIBRARY

W9-AQS-888

WITHDRAWN

RIVER FOREST PUBLIC LIBRARY
735 Lathrop Avenue
River Forest, Illinois 60305
708 / 366-5205

4/11

Make Your Own Art

Making Puppets

Sally Henry and Trevor Cook

PowerKiDS
press

New York

Published in 2011 by The Rosen Publishing Group, Inc.
29 East 21st Street, New York, NY 10010

Copyright © 2011 Arcturus Publishing Limited

All rights reserved. No part of this book may be reproduced in any form without permission in writing from the publisher, except by a reviewer.

Text and design: Sally Henry and Trevor Cook
Editor: Joe Harris
U.S. editor: Kara Murray
Photography: Sally Henry and Trevor Cook

Library of Congress Cataloging-in-Publication Data

Henry, Sally.
  Making puppets / by Sally Henry and Trevor Cook.
     p. cm. — (Make your own art)
  Includes index.
  ISBN 978-1-4488-1584-5 (library binding) — ISBN 978-1-4488-1615-6 (pbk.) —
ISBN 978-1-4488-1616-3 (6-pack)
  1. Puppet making—Juvenile literature. I. Cook, Trevor, 1948- II. Title.
  TT174.7.H45 2011
  745.592'24—dc22
                            2010024761

Printed in the United States

SL001623US

CPSIA Compliance Information: Batch #WA11PK: For Further Information contact Rosen Publishing, New York, New York at 1-800-237-9932

Contents

Introduction

Puppets come in all shapes and sizes. From wooden puppets in Europe, to the delicate shadow puppets of Indonesia, all explore the world of the imagination. You can make puppets as complicated or as simple as you like. The stick puppet theater on pages 28–30 takes a while to make and uses lots of different skills, while the sock puppet on pages 12–13 can be up and running almost in seconds. You just need to add your imagination!

Puppets from the Swedish Cottage Marionette Theater, in Central Park, in New York City.

Soft materials

Several of the puppet projects are made of soft materials. The sock puppets on pages 12–13 and the finger puppets on pages 8–9 are both made with **felt** or **fun foam**. These materials are easy to use because they can be cut with scissors, but won't fray. They come in bright colors and can be bought from craft stores.

fun foam and felt

rubber cement

Sometimes you may want to use a needle and thread to hold things together securely, but you can also use rubber cement to hold soft materials together.

It's strong enough to glue together the seams of the glove puppet on pages 14–15, and the funny bird's head and body on pages 22–23.

Tracing paper

Most of our templates are full size, so they can be copied by tracing. Put some **tracing paper** over the thing you want to copy. Go over the drawing with a soft pencil. Then transfer the drawing onto the new material by turning the tracing over, placing it face down on the new surface, and drawing firmly over the lines again. The pencil line should rub off onto the surface.

Where the drawings have been reduced in size, we've given the important measurements. Just follow these and draw freehand onto paper.

tracing paper

Glue

We've used a glue called **white glue** for many of our projects. It's white, but it turns clear when it dries. It's very good for sticking paper, card stock, and even wood. See the stick puppets on pages 28–30.

To stick paper to paper or paper to card stock, we sometimes use a **glue stick**. It's quick and clean but not really as permanent as white glue.

glue stick

white glue

Food stuffs

Many things around the kitchen can come in handy for craft projects. For example, the nutty professor (see pages 24–25) is made of **salt**, **cornstarch**, **peppercorns**, and **pasta**, and we've used **food coloring** and water to paint him.

When cooking is required, as for our dough (see pages 24–25), we strongly recommend that you get an adult to help you.

Joining things together

We used ordinary twine, a kind of string, for making the tinsel clown (pages 16–17), so that it would show up clearly in the pictures. However you may want to use **nylon line** instead. Even the thinnest kinds of nylon string are strong enough to hold up our puppet. This will make it very hard to see the strings! You can get it in short lengths from craft stores.

string

Barbecue skewers are ideal for making stick and shadow puppets. Get an adult to trim off the sharp points with a knife before you start.

nylon line

barbecue skewers

shadow puppet theater

stick puppet theater

Theaters

Most of our puppets work absolutely anywhere, but some really need a place to perform. The shadow puppets need somewhere you can make shadows, and the stick puppets need a way of hiding their sticks! We're going to use cardboard boxes for our theaters. They don't cost anything, they're adaptable, and they're a good place to store your puppets when you're not using them!

Paint and varnish

Any water-based **paint** can be used for painting your puppets. Bright colors often work best when painted thinly on a white background.

When the color is dry, make your work even brighter and protect it from damage by giving it a coat of **varnish**. Water-based household varnishes are fine. For delicate paper finishes, like the stick puppets, a special paper varnish is ideal. Jumping Jack, on pages 26–27, would look great with glossy varnish.

water-based paints

Card stock and cardboard

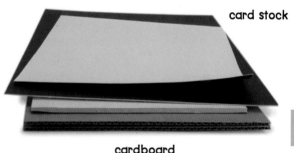

card stock

We've made puppets from **card stock** and the theaters are made from **cardboard**. Card stock is bendable, like thick paper, while cardboard is thicker, stronger, and harder, and is often made of layers of card stock.

cardboard

Manipulation

Manipulation is how you make your puppets move. Look at the expressions you can make with the simplest of our puppets, the sock puppet (pages 12–13). Whichever puppet you are working with, train your hands and practice as much as you can.

Clean and safe

When you're making your puppets, you need **somewhere to work** that's easy to clean. Glue is hard to get off fur and fabrics, so avoid rugs, curtains, and pets. A kitchen is an ideal place, but be sure to ask first. Sometimes there's other work being done there! Put sheets of newspaper down to protect work surfaces. Also, before you start, it's a good idea to prepare somewhere to put things while they dry.

Finger Puppets

Finger puppets are very quick to make and lots of fun to play with.

15 MINUTES

2 MINUTES

You will need:

- *Fun foam and felt in several colors*
- *Pins • Sequins*
- *Pencil • Scissors • Ruler*
- *Rubber cement • Googly eyes*

What to do...

Copy or trace our full-size outline patterns onto paper. Pin them to the fabric and cut around them. We've shown how to make the flower in steps. Make the rabbit, bear, and bird in the same way.

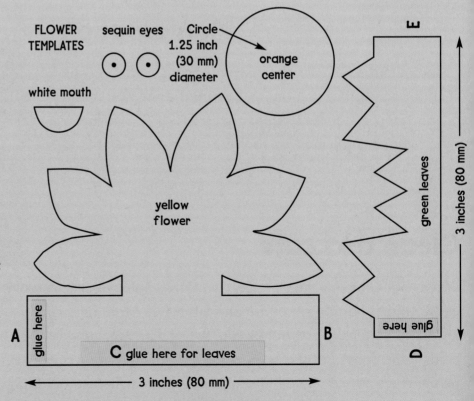

FLOWER TEMPLATES

sequin eyes

Circle 1.25 inch (30 mm) diameter

orange center

white mouth

yellow flower

green leaves

E

3 inches (80 mm)

glue here

A

C glue here for leaves

B

glue here

D

3 inches (80 mm)

To make the flower, trace the templates and carefully cut out three pieces of felt with scissors.

Wrap the yellow piece around and glue **A** to **B** with rubber cement. Stick on the orange center.

Wrap the green leaves around the base and glue at **C**, **D**, and **E**.

Add sequins for eyes and a small half circle of white felt for a smiley mouth. Now that you've got the idea, you can make the other creatures too!

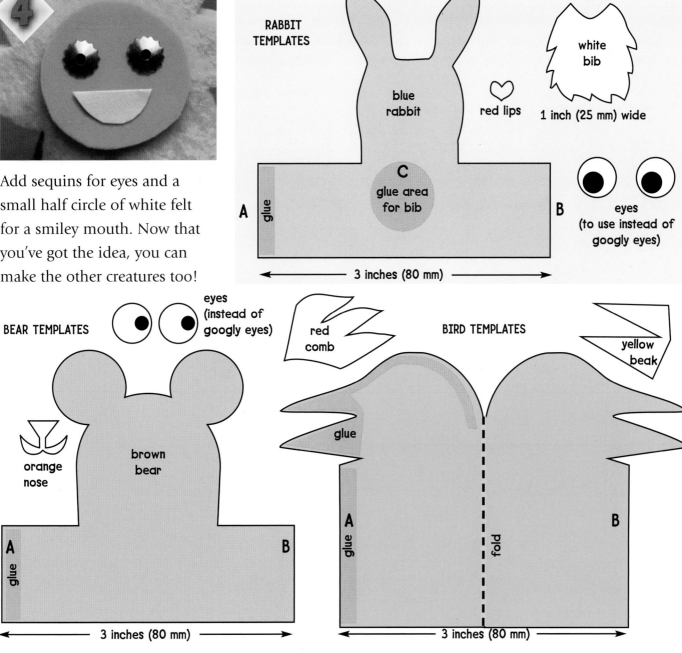

RABBIT TEMPLATES

blue rabbit

C
glue area for bib

A
glue

B

red lips

white bib
1 inch (25 mm) wide

eyes (to use instead of googly eyes)

3 inches (80 mm)

9

BEAR TEMPLATES

eyes (instead of googly eyes)

orange nose

brown bear

A
glue

B

3 inches (80 mm)

red comb

BIRD TEMPLATES

yellow beak

glue

A
glue

fold

B

3 inches (80 mm)

Walking Puppets

These charming finger puppets can walk, run, or even tap-dance!

20 MINUTES

10 MINUTES

You will need:

• *Hard card stock*
• *Scissors* • *Craft knife*
• *Colored marker pens or paints and brushes*
• *A black marker pen*

What to do...

Copy our templates for the puppets, making sure that the holes are big enough for your fingers. You can change their clothes and hairstyles if you like. Now let your fingers do the walking!

1

Copy these outlines onto your card stock.

PUPPET TEMPLATES

2

Color your puppets with marker pens or paints.

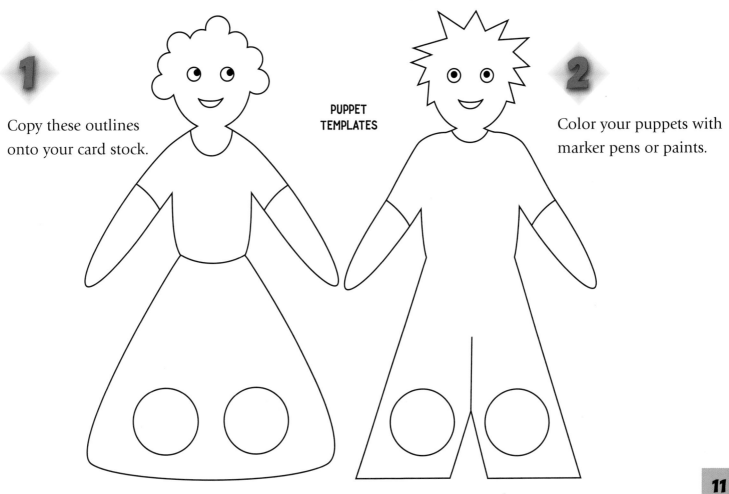

3

When your puppets are dry, draw in their eyes and mouths with a black marker.

4

Cut around your puppets with scissors. Ask an adult to cut out the finger holes with a craft knife.

5

Now it's time to dream up some stories and act them out with your puppets!

Sock Puppets

Who would have guessed you could have this much fun with an old sock?

You will need:

- *Clean, spare socks*
- *Fun foam or felt*
- *Scissors • Rubber cement*
- *Buttons or stick-on googly eyes*

What to do...

Find a spare sock and add stick-on eyes. The rest is up to you! You can cut out fun foam noses, ears, mouths, and hair. But the real skill is in how you move them around. Look at the pictures opposite for some ideas!

15 MINUTES

2 MINUTES

1

HAT
TEMPLATES

To make a hat, cut out these shapes from fun foam or felt.

Glue the shapes together with rubber cement.

When you've finished, glue the hat to your sock!

2

EAR
TEMPLATE

Cut out two pieces.

Snip with scissors.

A   B

Wrap A over B and glue to shape the ear.

A

3

FACE
TEMPLATES

To make ears for your puppet, cut out two shapes in fun foam, snip as shown above, and stick **A** and **B** together. Glue the ears to your sock.

To make a face, cut out the felt shapes above and glue them with rubber cement. Or to make a simpler face, just glue on googly eyes (see below)!

Glove Puppet

Glove at first sight! It's easier than it looks to make a cute teddy puppet.

60 MINUTES

5 MINUTES

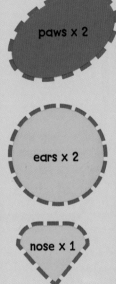

paws x 2

ears x 2

nose x 1

14

You will need:

- Fleece material and felt or fun foam
- Needle and thread • Dressmaker pins
- Circular sponge – about 4 inches (100 mm) in diameter • Two buttons
- Ribbon • Rubber cement
- Scissors • Pencil • Tracing paper

What to do...

You might need a little help from an adult with needles and pins when you make this puppet. Copy the template on the opposite page to make a paper pattern.

GLOVE PUPPET TEMPLATE

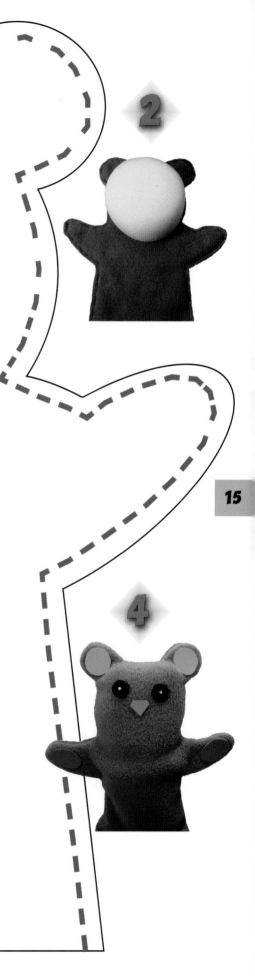

1 Pin this paper pattern to two layers of fabric, and carefully cut along the black line. Put the two shapes together, with the part of the fabric you want to be on the outside facing in. Now sew them together following the brown dotted line.

2 Glue a round sponge (trimmed to size if necessary) to the head area of the puppet with rubber cement. Allow it to dry completely.

3 Turn the puppet inside out, so that the seams are on the inside.

4 Working on the front of the puppet, the side with the sponge attached inside, sew on two buttons for eyes. Copy the nose, ear linings, and paw pad shapes on the opposite page in felt. Stick them all on with rubber cement. Finally, tie some ribbon in a big bow around its neck (see opposite).

↓ Leave this edge open.

15

Tinsel Clown

After a celebration, you usually take down the decorations and put them away. Here's how you can turn the end of a party into the beginning of a new project!

You will need:

- Foam craft ball –
  4 inches (100 mm) in diameter
- Soft plastic ball
- Cardboard • Ruler
- Two lengths of tinsel garland
  Red tinsel – 32 inches
  (800 mm)
  Blue tinsel – 20 inches (500 m
- Googly eyes • Scissors
- Clothes pins • Black marker
- String • Rubber cement • Penci
- Small plastic funnel

What to do...

You'd better get permission to use the decorations, before you get busy creating this happy clown. Twist the ruler to make him perform!

10
MINUTES

2
MINUTES

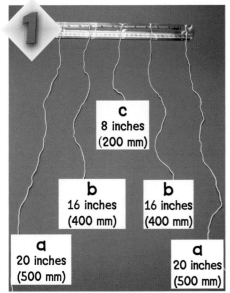

Tie five pieces of string to a ruler. The strings at each end of should be the longest (**a**), the one in the middle should be the shortest (**c**), and the other two should be a medium length (**b**).

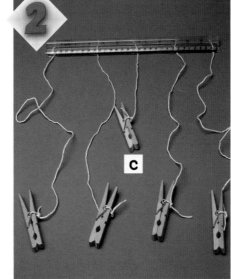

Tie clothes pins to the ends of each of the strings.

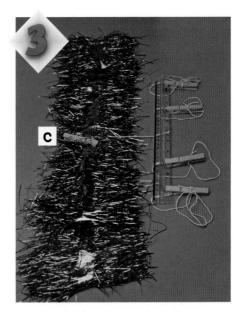

Take the red and blue tinsel garlands, and find the halfway point on each of them. Fix them together at this point with the clothes pin attached to the middle of the ruler (**c**).

eye position   eye position

CLOWN FACE
TEMPLATE

Cut 1 from
cardboard.

mustache   mustache

Clip the outer strings (**a**) to the ends of the red tinsel. Clip the medium strings (**b**) to the ends of the blue tinsel.

Copy the template and cut it out of cardboard. Ask an adult to cut a soft plastic ball in half with scissors. Stick on the nose with rubber cement. Draw in the mustache with a black marker. Stick on the eyes.

Make a hole in the head ball with a pencil and glue in the center string and clothes pin. Stick the face on the head with rubber cement. Glue on a funnel hat to finish!

Shadow Dragon

Shadow plays are a part of many cultures. Capture the drama of light and shade!

1 HOUR

10 MINUTES

You will need:

- Cardboard box • Tracing paper
- Hard black card stock • Paper fasteners
- Paint and brush • Tape
- Paper punch • Scissors • Craft knife
- Pen • Ruler • Pencil
- Barbecue skewers
- Desk lamp or big flashlight
- White glue

What to do...

Copy our templates of the dragon (on the opposite page) and the swordsman (on the left) onto black card stock. Connect them together with paper fasteners.

The cardboard box will become your theater. It should be at least 12 by 9 by 9 inches (300 x 230 x 230 mm).

DRAGON TEMPLATES

Cut holes with a paper punch.

D○

2 pieces

○A

B○

E○

D○

E○

2 pieces

○C

A○

D○

B○

E○

C○

paper fastener

1 Copy and cut out the shapes above and opposite. Put seven paper fasteners through the holes, joining **A** to **A**, **B** to **B**, and so on.

2 Glue the ends of the barbecue skewers where the green bars are shown. You can control your dragon by moving the ends of the sticks.

circular hole for lamp or flashlight

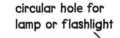

Draw a line about 2 inches (50 mm) from the edges.

3 Cut off the front and side flaps of the box with scissors. Mark a rectangle as shown above.

4 Ask an adult to cut holes at the front and back with a craft knife. Paint the outside of the box. Tape tracing paper inside the front to make the screen.

5 Shine a light toward the front and move your puppets close to the screen. Let the battle begin!

Napkin Puppets

Through the magic of puppetry, you can transform a simple napkin into a living creature!

2 HOURS

10 MINUTES

You will need:

- *Old clean, large napkins, or squares of light cloth*
- *Felt or fun foam • Thumbtacks • Pencil*
- *Foam craft balls, – 3 inches (75 mm) in diameter*
- *String • Card stock • Rubber cement*
- *Black marker pen • Rulers or similar pieces of wood*
- *Toothpick • An iron • Scissors • Glitter*
- *Paint and paintbrush*

What to do...

With just a head and two hands, you can do magic! Use movement to suggest a body that the audience can't see under the cloth. In all puppetry, the secret of success is plenty of practice!

1

TEMPLATE
for
HAND

Copy the hand template onto a piece of folded card and cut out two hands. Paint to match the face color of your puppet.

2

Allow paint to dry before gluing on features.

Make a head by painting a foam craft ball and gluing on shapes.

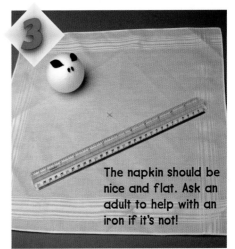

3

The napkin should be nice and flat. Ask an adult to help with an iron if it's not!

Lay out the napkin and find the middle. Glue the head in the middle with rubber cement and allow it to dry.

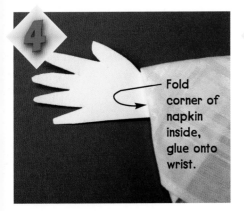

4

Fold corner of napkin inside, glue onto wrist.

Glue the hands in the corners of the cloth with rubber cement.

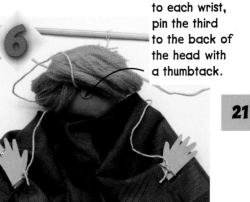

5

8 inches (200 mm) long

16 inches (400 mm) long

16 inches (400 mm) long

Tie three strings to the ruler or piece of wood.

Tie one string to each wrist, pin the third to the back of the head with a thumbtack.

6

21

Attach the other ends of the strings to the puppet.

7

Use half a toothpick for a baton!

We've used some black cloth and a white card stock shirt front to make this conductor puppet.

8

Her hair is yarn and her features are fun foam. Use glitter to turn this napkin into a ball gown!

9

This ghost is the quickest string puppet to make. Stick four black shapes on a foam ball.

Funny Bird

Follow these steps to make a dancing bird with big feet!

45 MINUTES

5 MINUTES

22

You will need:

- *Two foam craft balls about, 2 and 3 inches (50 and 75 mm) in diameter*
- *Colored feathers • Fun foam or felt • Elastic band*
- *Air-drying modeling clay*
- *Old jump rope or soft braided cord (to make legs and neck)*
- *Googly eyes • Chopsticks*
- *Four colored strings – two 12 inches (300 mm) long two 16 inches (400 mm) long*
- *Scissors • Pencil • Rubber cement*

What to do...

You may need an adult to help you with the strings if they need adjusting and with the rubber cement. Follow the steps to make a funny colorful puppet and enjoy learning how to operate it!

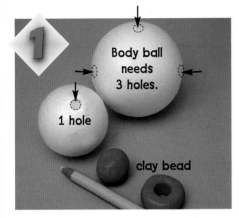

Make two balls of clay 1 inch (25 mm) across. Push the pencil through them to make them into beads.

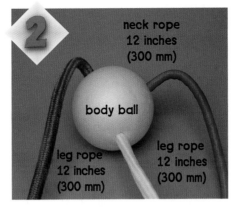

Put three holes in the body ball and one hole in the head ball with the pencil. Glue the ropes in the holes with rubber cement.

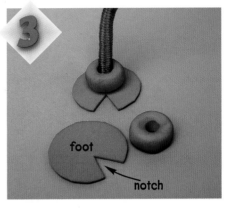

Cut two circles with notches from fun foam or felt. Stick the clay beads on the circles and to the ends of the leg ropes.

Stick the googly eyes on circles of fun foam. Cut the beak from yellow fun foam. Stick the pieces to the head with rubber cement.

Glue the ends of three feathers to the head. Glue more small feathers all over the body.

Stick larger tail feathers to the back end of the bird with rubber cement.

23

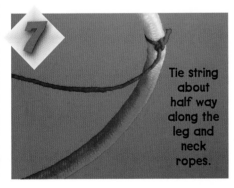

Tie strings to the legs and neck. Glue a string to the top of the bird's back.

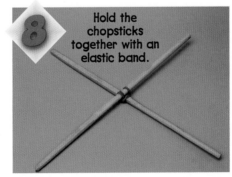

Fix the chopsticks in a cross shape. Tie the leg strings to the ends of one stick. Tie the neck and back strings to the other chopstick. Done!

Nutty Professor

Make this silly genius just using things from the kitchen!

60 MINUTES

10 MINUTES

You will need:

- 1 cup cornstarch • 1 cup salt
- ½ cup water • Saucepan
- Spoon • Fusilli (twisted pasta)
- Teaspoon • Scissors • Thick card stock • Large old napkin
- Black peppercorns • Rubber cement
- Food coloring • Paintbrush
- Two pieces of dowel (round wooden sticks) 8 by .25 inch (200 x 6 mm)
- Tracing paper • Pencil

What to do...

Here's an unusual puppet you work with two sticks! You may need an adult to help you with preparing the dough and fitting the professor's gown with rubber cement, but otherwise you just need to hunt around for some materials in the kitchen!

Put the cornstarch, salt, and water into a saucepan. Ask an adult to cook the liquid on a medium heat, stirring until it thickens.

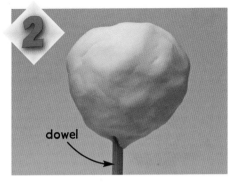

When the dough cools, knead it well. Make it into a ball and push a stick into it. Model the head and neck.

dowel

Push the pasta into the dough for hair and peppercorns for eyes. Mold bits of dough for the nose, cheeks, and ears.

Form a smiley mouth with a teaspoon.

Let the dough harden. Paint the face with a few drops of red and yellow food coloring mixed with a little water.

Fold an old napkin in four. Cut off the corner to make a hole in the middle big enough to go over the neck of the puppet.

Hold the head upside down, fit the napkin, and brush rubber cement around the neck. With the head the right way up, check that the napkin is glued neatly.

glue

25

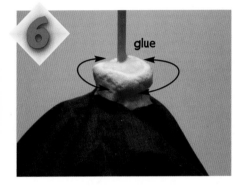

HAND TEMPLATE Cut two.

Copy the template. Cut two hands from thick card stock. Glue one hand to a stick.

Fold and stick the edge of the napkin over the wrist with the stick. Glue the loose hand to the other side of the napkin.

mustache

Now stick on a twisty pasta mustache under his nose and you have a nutty professor! Have fun with him!

Jumping Jack

Pull his string to see him jump. This little puppet can't keep still!

45 MINUTES

5 MINUTES

You will need:

- *Markers pens or paints and a brush*
- *Paper fasteners • Thumbtack*
- *Thick card stock • Gift ribbon*
- *Scissors • Hole punch • Large bead*
- *String*

What to do...

Jack is like a toy often made in wood, but he will jump just as well if you make him in thick card stock. Ask an adult to help you with the holes and the strings.

1 Copy all the parts (including the dots) of Jumping Jack on thick card stock.

2 Color all the parts with marker pens or water-based paints. Allow to dry completely.

Tie a loop of ribbon through this hole to hang Jack up with.

3 Carefully cut out the pieces with scissors.

4 Make holes on the red dots with a hole punch. Push a thumbtack through the green dots to make smaller holes. Protect your work surface with scrap card stock.

5 paper fastener

Adjust fasteners so that the joints are loose and free to move.

Join Jack together with six paper fasteners through the large holes on his body, arms, and legs.

6 Bend back the points of the paper fasteners.

Knot the ends of the string.

Turn the puppet over. Join the arms and legs together with string. Tie a long string to the short strings. Put a bead at the end of this string.

Stick Puppets

Here are some puppets with their own theater, made from a shoe box!

45 MINUTES

5 MINUTES

You will need:

- *Empty shoe box – about 13 by 8.5 by 4.5 inches (320 x 220 x 120 mm)*
- *Ruler*
- *Hard white card stock • Colored paper*
- *White glue • Barbecue skewers – about 12 inches (300 mm) long • Paint and brushes or colored markers • Black marker pens • Craft knife*
- *Scissors*

What to do...

We're going to make some stick puppets and their own theater out of an old shoe box. We've imagined a scene with a king, a queen, and a little prince and a big palace on a hill. You can make up a story about our little characters, or make up your own. Get some friends to help or just to watch!

1

Puppets are 2 to 3 inches (50–75 mm) high.

Make drawings like these on white card stock. Draw with a black marker pen. Color the puppets with paints or markers.

2

Cut out the puppets with scissors. Glue each one to the end of a barbecue skewer. Get an adult to trim off the sharp ends of the barbecue skewers with a craft knife.

3

Cut a slot at the back of the box, to almost the full width.

Cut two slots 2 inches (50 mm) from the back, about 4 inches (100 mm) long.

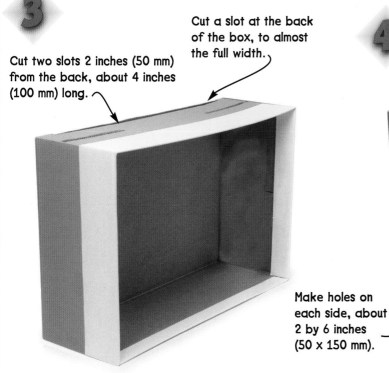

Make holes on each side, about 2 by 6 inches (50 x 150 mm).

Get an adult to help you make slots in your box with a craft knife. The scenery will fit in the slots so cut them neatly. Then paint them with a scene.

4

Cut a hole in the lid, about 1 inch (25 mm) in from the edge.

Cut a hole in the box lid and glue it back in place. Make holes in both ends for your puppets to get on and off the stage.

5

3 inches (75 mm) wide

Back drop 11 inches (280 mm) wide

3 inches (75 mm) wide

Scenery flats and backdrop should be 1 inch (25 mm) taller than your box.

Cut three pieces of card stock to fit into the slots in the box. Copy our scenery, cut a picture from a colored magazine, or draw and color your own set!

6

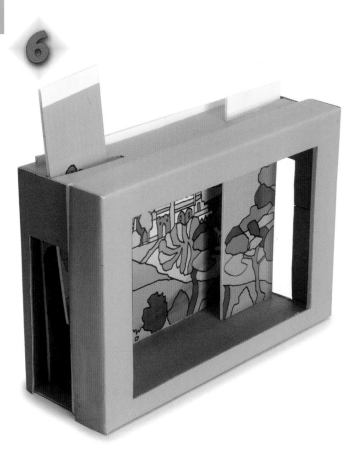

Fit the scenery in the box.

7

Cut out and glue on a little paper decoration.

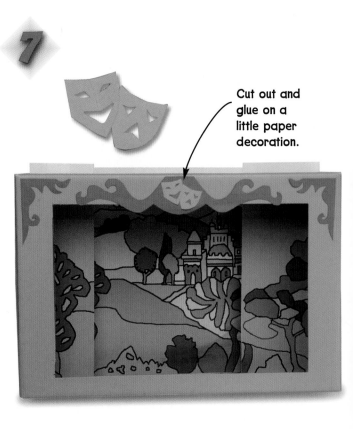

Your stick puppet theater is ready to go!

Glossary

audience (AH-dee-ints) A group of people watching a show or work of art.

baton (buh-TAHN) A thin stick used by conductors of an orchestra.

chopsticks (CHOP-stiks) A pair of wooden or plastic sticks used to eat Asian food.

decoration (deh-kuh-RAY-shun) Something added to an object to make it look pretty.

felt (FELT) Nonwoven material made from wool that does not fray when cut.

flats (FLATS) Flat pieces of scenery used at the sides of the stage in a theater.

googly eyes (GOO-glee EYEZ) Plastic stick-on eyes with moving parts, used for making toys.

professor (preh-FEH-ser) A university teacher.

scenery (SEE-neh-ree) Backgrounds, usually painted to provide a setting for a play in a theater.

seams (SEEMZ) The lines formed by sewing together two pieces of cloth.

sequin (SEE-kwun) A small shiny disk stuck onto clothing for decoration.

set (SET) A collection of scenery used in a scene for a play in the theater.

template (TEM-plut) An exact version of something that makes it easy to make many copies.

tinsel (TINT-sel) A decoration made in strings and garlands from very shiny plastic shreds.

tracing paper (TRAYS-ing PAY-per) A special kind of paper that lets you see a picture through it and has a surface that you can draw on in ink or pencil.

varnish (VAHR-nish) A special liquid made to put on a surface that then dries and protects.

Index

Web Sites

Due to the changing nature of Internet links, PowerKids Press has developed an online list of Web sites related to the subject of this book. This site is updated regularly. Please use this link to access the list:
www.powerkidslinks.com/myoa/puppet/